Upgrade

Home Extensions, Alterations and Refurbishments

gestalten

How to marry the practical with the poetic

RECYCLING IN ARCHITECTURE GOES
far beyond the simple reuse of materials. Whole buildings, sections of them, or even just their floor plans are being retained, refurbished, transformed, or extended into living spaces fit for modern purposes—everything from a lofty home among the silos of a former cement factory, to a dizzying dwelling in a Dutch water tower, to a lovingly constructed minimalist playhouse in a 1920s dove cote. Though we as a species have always carefully constructed our surroundings, a practice deeply rooted in an awareness of the past (whether through materials, knowledge, nostalgia, or techniques, to name just a few), some structures reveal fragments of their histories while cleverly incorporating the necessities of contemporary life—

... and it is these buildings that are particularly fascinating in today's reuse-recycle-reduce culture. And yet, we often hear that we live in a time that has no respect for the past: that ours is an era that disregards the architectural qualities of previous eras in an often flagrant way.

But the huge array of rebuilds, conservation projects, and thoughtful extensions existing today suggest otherwise. One might say we are living in a golden era, where architects are responding to a broad change in attitude toward our built history. After all, it is only relatively recently that we created institutions to protect not just famous historical buildings but also more quotidian structures: in 1988 that the Monumentwet allowed the Netherlands' heritage authority to take a significantly more active role in the preservation of the nation's cultural heritage; Portugal's IPA, the Inventory of Architectural Heritage, was only established in the 1990s. We are realizing that domestic buildings are as much a part of our heritage as palaces or museums.

And what matters most is how we choose to reflect upon and use that heritage; most of all, we have come to understand that respect for the past does not necessarily have to mean slavish adulation or imitation. Spanning the rural to the urban—with mountain chalets, cottages, and barn conversions in between—this book explores how existing buildings can be extended (new added to old), refurbished (an updated interior with an untouched exterior), or completely rebuilt in order to create new possibilities for living, whether in a recent ruin high in the Italian Alps, a lime-built cottage that features lovingly preserved cracks on a remote Scottish isle, or a rear extension to a Victorian terraced house in a London suburb.

Existing buildings simply offer different opportunities to architects than new-build projects. For instance, the shell of an eighteenth-century house on the side of an extinct volcano in the Azores was retained not out of mere fancy—nor because heritage restrictions may have prevented the construction of a brand-new house in its place—but because it already sat in the right position, captured wonderful views, and was formed from the same basalt rock as the island itself. Roofs became decks for seating and the house was adapted into a comfortable, modern home. Working with existing buildings can turn architecture into an archaeological practice; we can discover what we have become through the ways we choose to change the past. Whether architects are simply building extensions—where it is clear where the new section meets the old—or making complete interior refurbishments or alterations with major changes inside and outside,

... they are setting in motion an act of double imagination: how did people live in this house once? How might they live in it again?

Despite the proliferation of converted buildings, society at large continues to work within the logic of disposability—use it up, throw it out, and replace it with something entirely new. It is perhaps this attitude that gives heritage buildings their heightened appeal, amidst a sea of contemporary structures that all look alike. With some creativity, know-how, and investment (time, money, or both), existing structures or materials can be adapted to particular needs and turned into a unique achievement. With these projects, firms like Pictet Architectes are able to take the necessary time and care to make sensitive decisions about every aspect of conservation—clearly visible in their renovation of a chalet in the Pays-d'Enhaut. We love to retain and reuse things; we enjoy the curves of ancient walls and the warmth of ancient timbers, even as we enjoy modern amenities. When traces of the past are not hidden from view but exposed in a carefully thought out way, we can enrich our personal experiences in the places we call home.

Naturally, remnants of the past take on different proportions in different projects. Materials and techniques that are no longer widely used—the notched

WHERE TO FIND:

Opposite page:
Refurbished by SAMI-Arquitectos, E/C House in basalt and concrete stands on Pico Island in the Azores, Portugal (see pp. 242–49).

single-family houses, which in turn has led to a broader reinvigoration of old urban areas.

Above all, this book celebrates the unique way that architecture marries the practical with the poetic; we celebrate the work of architects like Haworth Tompkins, who can eke out space for an artist from a dovecote while simultaneously making their own artistic statement. Of course, these structures—most often homes but occasionally also places for work or play—must provide modern levels of comfort and a series of spaces that accomodate the clients' lifestyle needs and wishes. There are all kinds of technical challenges and possibilities that arise in the work of renovation and conversion—as seen in the profiles and interviews in the pages ahead—but these buildings have been selected because they also say something about the past as well as the present—often in surprising and unique ways.

Whether a French dwelling with a sixteenth-century heart and a patchwork history, a deconsecrated Dutch church with modular rooms, or a canal-side factory in northern Portugal, most of the projects outlined here are found in Europe. This concentration is possibly thanks to the sheer number of existing buildings on the continent and the comparative lack of space in which to build anew. Likewise, stringent heritage-protection legislation in Western Europe has created an architectural culture that champions innovation and creative solutions. Across the continent, a huge variety of restorations can be found—constructions that were originally industrial buildings, farms, barns, or even houses—and the variety extends to how the structures have been made over: from minimal interventions on the interior to radical alterations of not only the structure in question but the very idea of building itself.

...No matter how the individual examples have been transformed, each has been imbued with the love of building and making once again.

wood of a Nordic cabin, for example—can be juxtaposed with contemporary shapes or favored materials, like blackened timber, to form a whole that does not feel disjointed. A single component such as a polished concrete floor or a weathering-steel extension can add as much to the old as the old adds to the new. These physical contrasts add singular touches and atmosphere to both interior and exterior.

... In a world where we fear that craftsmanship is disappearing, we often feel the need to capture it so it might be appreciated anew.

The beautiful, latticed woodwork of the Köhler Pavilion by Trodahl Arkitekter would be a crime to lose. To take a ruin, or an otherwise obsolete structure and bring it back to life is an act not just of respect, but one of understanding the skills of the past. Not simply copying but rather being invigorated and inspired by the spirit and excellence of the workmanship. This attitude has produced so many practicioners in Europe and beyond who are fiercely committed to the preservation of historic structures—not simply because of their symbolic value but because the existing building is a vessel that holds valuable resources. The culture of preservation is about valuing materials and the craftsmanship that has gone into their manipulation as much as their historic value.

At the other end of the spectrum are buildings in tight urban sites and executed on a very limited budget. The work of Jonathan Tuckey, for example, is often about finding the potential in London's local typologies, such as the terraced house or the tenement block, and adapting them to new needs; in doing so, they celebrate the clarity and vitality of the original work. Likewise Zecc Architecten and GRAUX & BAEYENS architecten have been prompted by the influx of new people to the cities of Utrecht and Ghent, which boast a large number of nineteenth-century houses. The new demands of contemporary lives have led to innovative

WHERE TO FIND:

Opposite page:
Ricardo Bofill's La Fábrica: a restored concrete factory in Catalonia, Spain (see pp. 88–93).

Top:
Inside a railway cottage in Santpoort, the Netherlands, which was renovated and extended by Zecc Architecten (see pp. 106–11).

Above:
The interior of the Old Catholic Church of St. James in Utrecht by Zecc Architecten (see pp. 94–101).

BRICK WORKS
in Northern Berlin
Asdfg Architekten

Dates from: 1844
BERLIN, GERMANY

Before modification

Formerly a miller's house,
a police station and a
workshop, the house—built
in 1844—has had multiple
uses and is the oldest
building in the Berlin
district of Prenzlauer Berg.

WHEN THE PLANNING AUTHORITIES insisted that asdfg Architekten reconstruct the facade of a heritage-protected miller's house, part of a thorough redevelopment of the oldest building in Berlin's fashionable Prenzlauer Berg district, the designers were left in a quandary. They considered reconstructing the facade precisely as depicted in an 1844 drawing. But while they wanted to engage with the history of the building, they didn't want to pretend that the facade was the 170-year-old original.

Architects in these situations are often compelled to consider a more artistic version of truth than a scientific one, and thus the stone pattern on the historical drawing was rendered as a pattern in the new plaster facade. It is not pretending to be real, but it acknowledges what once was real.

Internally, the building had been subdivided so many times that it was hard to tell what was even authentic anymore, save for the external walls. These elements, apart from one structural brick wall, are all that was →

Alterations to the brickwork have not been disguised, and the interior space was made as generous and open as possible.

kept of the original. Alterations to the brick work have not been disguised, and the interior space was made as generous and open as possible, allowing the family to experience the fabric of the building as its real character, rather than a facsimile of what it once was. _____

THINKING
Through the Rafters
GENS

Dates from: mid-20th century
ZUTZENDORF, ALSACE, FRANCE

From the exterior, the home
is very conventional;
inside, it is anything but.

THERE APPEARS TO HAVE BEEN
very little rebuilding in this contemporary version of a suburban Alsatian home. The only preexisting component incorporated into the new building was a wall: one poorly built from concrete block that had once fenced off the courtyard. Even this single element was a significant launching point for the new structure—whose construction is admittedly far better executed than the original wall. The concrete block walls and in situ concrete for the ground floor are of the highest quality, providing the foundation for the wooden framework roof structure clad in tiles above.

This project is in many ways the rebuild of an architectural typology. As the architects say of the planning culture of this Alsatian village: "Do as your neighbor does, and all the neighbors will agree." The building by GENS architects is effectively a rethinking or repurposing of a local house type, characterized by the tile-covered gabled roof. The ground floor is free space, totally opened up to the south-facing garden. Above what is effectively a ground-floor apartment is another space: a retreat hidden in the industrial wooden rafters that support the roof. From the exterior, this home is very conventional; inside, it is anything but. _____

Optimizing LEAN SPACE
Dierendonck-blancke Architects

Dates from: early 20th Century
GHENT, BELGIUM

THIS TINY, TERRACED HOUSE SITS on a narrow plot in the historic center of Ghent. The street on which it stands is lined with various types of row houses, each with a different cornice height, roof shape, or building line. In this eclectic streetscape, Dierendonckblancke have created a modern house, adapted from the brick original. This new structure now provides a workshop for the owner on the ground floor and a two-story apartment on the upper floors.

Space is at a premium here: wooden staircases between the new wooden floors are narrow while the terrace to the rear has been optimized to incorporate extra external space on two different levels. Sitting below a slightly pitched roof, the top floor accommodates two bedrooms and a bathroom. The new wooden frame, which expands the house closer to the street, is left unclad. This use of untreated wood is a beautiful, rustic feature and lends unique character to the interior space; it also optimizes —even if by mere millimeters—the interior space.

The outer shell is kept as thin as possible too: the PVC membrane—just two millimeters thick—envelopes both the roof and original brick facades. The overall effect is a lean, muscular house with a great deal of character. _____

Before renovation began, this sixteenth-century house was uninhabited for 25 years. The different styles of masonry seen on the facade were the result of sections being added at various points in history.

COLLAGING
Old and New
Galletti & Matter
Architects

Dates from: 16th century
VALAIS, SWITZERLAND

Before modification

The original stone structure has been kept, but it has been reinforced with wood, steel, and concrete components.

THE TOWN OF SION

is one of the most important prehistoric settlements in Europe. The original building that Galletti & Matter Architects have refurbished may not be nearly as old—in fact, it is a patchwork of different historical ages with a sixteenth-century heart—but their rebuild is as much an archaeological gesture as it is architectural. Closer study of the house led to the hypothesis that the southern area was originally for human inhabitation, whilst the northern part was probably used for animals at some stage, although this was subsequently used to house humans as well.

The house, which had been abandoned for 25 years, was a wreck when they began. It has since been split into two apartments, keeping the idea of having two separate parts—the north and south—in one building. The original stone structure has been preserved to maintain the structural integrity, but it has been reinforced with wood, steel, and concrete components. These elements not only support the building but provide a visual update, mixing flavors of the present day into an already-beguiling collage of past building techniques. Here, terracotta tiling, reinforced concrete, and black steel have been added to stone and painted wood. _____

This view of the northwest facade illustrates the house's two-part structure. During the two-year alteration, the original structure was kept, so as not to weaken the house.

From Useless Space to SUNLIGHT MAGNET
Rise Design Studio

Dates from: 1870
LONDON, UNITED KINGDOM

LIKE MANY SIMILAR HOUSES, this Victorian dwelling in London was given a two-story rectilinear extension—not quite the width of the original house—sometime in the early twentieth century, not long after it was built. This type of extension is often described as an "outrigger," which usually did not extend to the boundary wall, in order to allow the delivery of coal into the heart of the house. Because a contemporary city dweller has little need for coal, these alleys have become a useless feature. This property had remained untouched for a long time, due in part to these anachronistic features as well as the home's inefficient layout and lack of natural light. The extension and renovation improved the quality of light and opened up the ground floor interior to allow for easy access between the kitchen, living room, and rear garden. The side alley has been enclosed by a frameless glazed envelope, which allows for views to the garden and lets natural light flood the building. Instead of designating spaces by walls, contrasting floor materials are used to distinguish between the three main areas; encaustic tiles greet you upon entering the house, distressed oak flooring is used in the reception rooms, and polished concrete for the open-plan kitchen. _____

Instead of designating spaces by walls, contrasting floor materials are used to distinguish between the three main areas.

OPEN
Planning
Maxwan

Dates from: ca. 1900
GELDERMALSEN, THE NETHERLANDS

THE ARCHITECTS MAXWAN
were initially asked to help their clients
realize their dream of a large open-
plan kitchen and living room for an
early-twentieth-century barn they had
already converted themselves, located
on a beautiful site bordering the River
Linge. The owners wanted a space
where they could entertain friends and
that they could use for work functions,
as the barn was both their home and
office. The barn had been extended
in the 1990s, with a simple 10-meter
extrusion over two floors. However,
this previous extension had left the
masonry barn with virtually no relation
to the beautiful landscape surrounding the house. →

Maxwan went beyond the brief of their kitchen refurbishment and proposed an inversion in the layout of the house.

Most of the openings in the building's facades were either too small, in the wrong place, or both. Maxwan went beyond the brief of their kitchen refurbishment and proposed an inversion in the layout of the house, moving the offices and storage space to the extension and returning the private spaces to the old barn. A large slit was cut into the barn roof to let in light. The final touch was a long, continuous timber insertion in ash wood to serve as kitchen, storage, stairs, and library all at once. _____

Unearthing Layers of ARCHITECTURAL MEMORY
Tsuruta Architects

Dates from: early 20th century
LONDON, UNITED KINGDOM

WHEN AN ARCHITECT BUILDS in a city these days, they are invariably placing a new layer upon other layers. The original extension of this early-twentieth-century Victorian terraced house, although it had no distinct historical or architectural value, had a pitched-roof profile typical of garden houses from that period. The architects chose to incorporate this form into the new facade of the rear garden—hoping to preserve the structure's charm or provoke an associated memory. →

Before modification

The architects have carried forward an exploration of memory into the reconstruction.

The architects have carried forward an exploration of memory into the reconstruction, too. The structures of the new envelope have been exposed internally wherever practically possible, so that the future stories of the house will be inscribed into its surfaces. Marks from the bare plaster finish are left exposed in the bedrooms, while the slow patination of the bespoke copper and brass fittings will display the passage of time as they change from their original color.

Because the extension increased the depth of the house, a two-story light well was added between the new and the original parts of the building, in order to bring more natural light into interior rooms. The light well serves as a focal point in the home, connecting the kitchen and dining level with the bedrooms.

The light well serves as a focal point in the home, connecting the kitchen and dining level with the bedrooms.

Reupholster, Repanel, RESTORE

Fraher Achitects

Dates from: 1820s
LONDON, UNITED KINGDOM

MANY MODEST BRICK-BUILT, two-story terraced houses were developed for artisan workers in London in the nineteenth century. This one in particular had been unoccupied for ten years and was run down. The dilapidated building required extensive refurbishment with a sensitive approach. Restoring the fireplaces walls, architraves, and skirting to their original condition brought the building back to its original design. The addition of a contemporary rear and side extension complements these features and updates the building. A large, open-plan living space creates a new light and airy space; a new glass roof extension feeds light into the whole plan of the building.

Arrangements of modern furniture update the traditional spaces. Many antique chairs were refurbished and reupholstered, while minimalist light fittings complement the interior. Materiality was very important to help produce a sensitive contemporary design, while also assisting the conservationist approach. European oak was used where shelving was required. _____

The dilapidated building required extensive refurbishment with a sensitive approach.

Materiality was very important to help produce a sensitive contemporary design, while also assisting the conservationist approach.

A Hybridized VISION for Ghent
GRAUX & BAEYENS architecten

BASED IN GHENT, BELGIUM

The dilapidated industrial heritage of northern European port cities like Ghent—the empty warehouses and abandoned docks—is often intriguing and can even be beautiful. However, they often seduce us into a narrative about life in these places that is not based in truth. While this abandoned infrastructure suggests a narrative of industrial and social decline, it often belies a very different, often opposite reality. While the city center of Ghent is historic and medieval, the wider city has always embraced growth and innovation, and thus is a relatively big city for Belgium—although small in comparison to Paris, or even Brussels.

Ghent is a city that is growing fast. As with many European cities, its historic center was depopulated during the 1970s and '80s. However, in the 1990s, the population started to pick up again and was booming by the turn of the millennium. The city has a large quantity of row houses between two and four stories high. Due to increasing demand for housing, prices have risen in recent years and continue to do so, with these town houses being particularly popular among young couples and small families. According to the architect Basile Graux, founding partner of GRAUX & BAEYENS, this arrangement presents a challenge and an opportunity. "A large part of the budget goes to the purchase of the property and leaves only the possibility to refurbish," he says.

This is the case with House G-S, which sits in the heart of Muide; a formerly working-class neighborhood in the port district to the north of Ghent. The nineteenth-century corner house is of particular value because of the singular view it offers toward the old city harbor docks. The house's prominent position lent itself well to a sculptural response. Renovation began as an almost aggressive stripping back of the original house to its very essence, represented—so the architects

thought—by the facade, the stairwell, and the structural components of the roof, which together envelope the new spaces created within.

But the conversion is not a simple recreation of the former house. Partly to take advantage of the view across the water and partly to provide more open social spaces, the architects have inverted the functional arrangement of the conventional terraced house. In the new house, the bedrooms are located on the ground floor and the living spaces are located on the first floor, while the kitchen and dining room occupy the top floor and provide access to an adjacent, enclosed roof garden/patio. In doing so, the architects have transformed this nineteenth-century Belgian corner house into a hybrid of contemporary and historical style.

Far from hiding this juxtaposition between old and new, the house celebrates it. Set within the rough-textured yet equally familiar facade, the

black-tinted windows are the first sign of this play of contrasts. On top of the husk of the old building, a white sculptural plug sits on top, evoking and adding to the roof pattern of the adjacent properties. A series of new windows have been punctured into the walls of the old building, chosen based on the view they provide. Inside the house, the brick walls have been simply rendered in gray and black, contrasting with the new, bespoke monochrome-white furniture.

Although the building provides a very particular experience on the interior, giving the clients a private world most unlike that of an unconverted property, it is rightly—given its prominent position—a very public realization of the relationship between the historic fabric of the city and those that now live and work there. Instead of an enclosed, claustrophobic series of rooms, the living spaces are arranged as a stack of volumes. The guarded delineation of areas into →

In House G-S, a nineteenth-century corner house in Ghent, GRAUX & BAEYENS have turned a conventional terraced house upside down, putting the bedrooms on the ground floor.

"Ghent has, in our opinion, a good balance between old and new, restored and refurbished buildings."

Basile Graux

Before modification

their varying degrees of private space has been replaced by an open plan, which—bedrooms aside—makes the entire house open to visitors.

For Basile Graux, who studied along with his partner Koen Baeyens at Sint-Lucas (now known as KU Leuven) in Ghent, it is clearly a response to the wider architectural cultural of the city. "Ghent has, in our opinion, a good balance between old

and new, restored and refurbished buildings," he says. "If the city wants to keep evolving it has to leave room for regeneration. Therefore, it has to allow for transformation and even embrace this."

Not that this is a strategy unique to the city of Ghent. From among their other work, the KCV house, involving the renovation of a slightly older building into a three-story family house in

the old center of Mechelen, is worth comparing to House G-S. The building in Mechelen is cramped and enclosed on three sides by adjacent structures, so the architects' intervention prioritized a radical alteration of the street facade, providing light and views to the front of the house. Previously, a series of small windows defined the facade. But by stacking new large, square windows, which are almost the width of →

Far from hiding the juxtaposition between old and new, House G-S celebrates it.

the new facade and the height of each story, it projects the interior beyond the building in a theatrical fashion, a common feature of their work.

Certainly, their output as a practice is incredibly diverse in terms of architecture, but one can also see that there is a similarity in approach across the entirety of their oeuvre. "We believe that every project will be different if you ask the right questions. We are searching for clarity and balance that results in one clear formal idea," says Graux. _____

The guarded delineation of areas has been replaced by an open-plan, which—bedrooms aside—makes the entire house open to visitors.

Like a sculpture placed inside an existing container, the rooms and living spaces are "stacked" and have sections cut out for views.

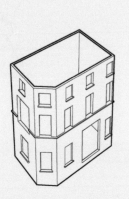
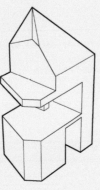

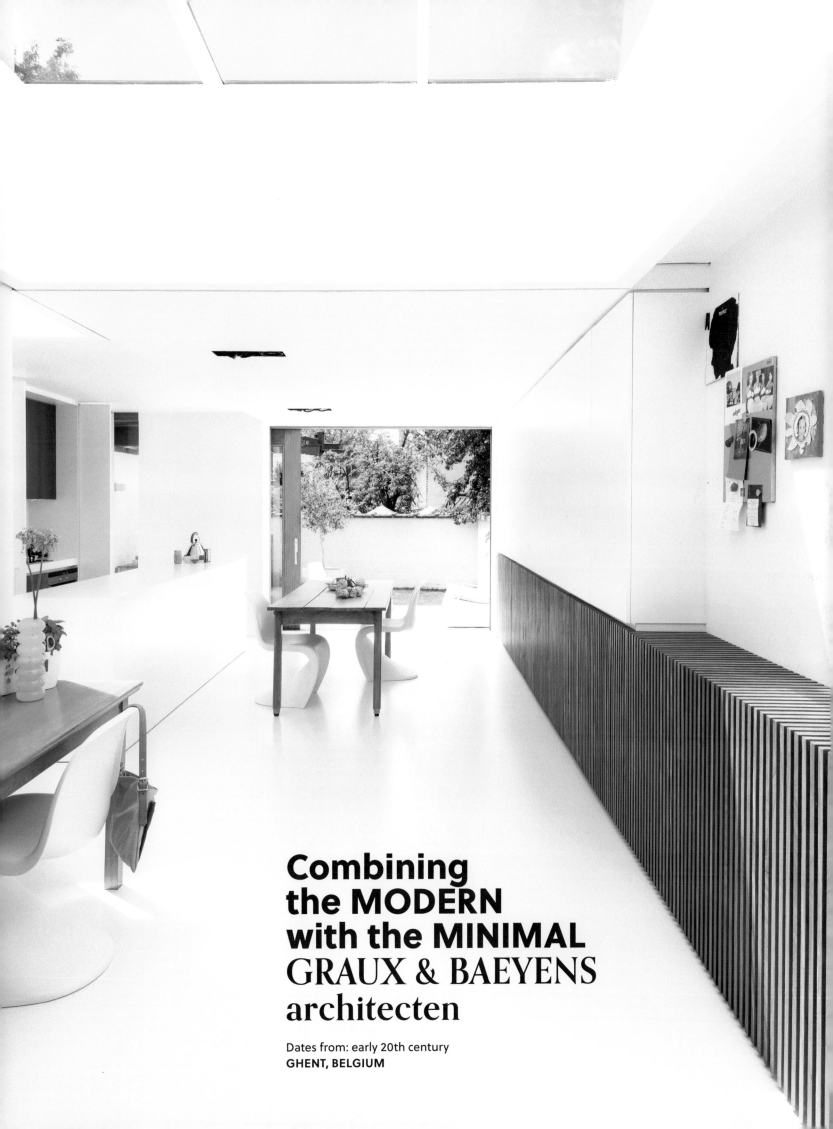

Combining
the MODERN
with the MINIMAL
GRAUX & BAEYENS
architecten

Dates from: early 20th century
GHENT, BELGIUM

Before modification

GRAUX & BAEYENS designed the structure at the back of the house to allow in light. The multi-purpose room also connects the interior to the exterior with sliding windows.

ALTHOUGH AGAIN BASED in Ghent, this extension of a kitchen into a long, multipurpose space that stretches out into the garden has a great deal in common with the terraced houses in London included in this book. The existing kitchen no longer met the needs of the client but was sufficient in scale to accommodate the new concept.

The starting point for House W-DR was to create a new multipurpose room which maximizes the inhabitants' sense of space. The room is effectively designed to accommodate a key piece of furniture, the massive dining/work table, which provides a central platform upon which daily life can be planned and enacted. Two horizontal frames in the roof allow →

The starting point was to create a new multipurpose room which maximizes the inhabitants' sense of space.

light deep into the existing house and offer a new view to the rear. The windows with a garden view can slide fully open. The boundary between the kitchen and the garden has been further blurred by using the same floor decking externally and internally. There are great architectural gestures in this house, but the subtle interventions that allow light to filter into the space are perhaps its greatest achievement. _____

A Practical
and Sculptural
INTERVENTION
GRAUX & BAEYENS
architecten

Dates from: 19th century
GHENT, BELGIUM

In a vacant shell, the architects inserted what they call—rather harshly—"three black monoliths."

THIS IS ANOTHER OF THE TYPICAL row houses built in the nineteenth century that lie in a ring around the medieval heart of Ghent. The conversion could be considered quite unusual, largely based on the slightly unusual needs that the couple who owned the house had for the ground floor area. Both were avid mountain bike riders and wanted a space in which they could both work on their bikes but also relax. Graux & Baeyens realized very quickly that the previous room divisions on the floor would have to go, and they stripped the ground and first floor back, removing all partition walls to create an open plan.

In the vacant shell, the architects inserted what they call—rather harshly—"three black monoliths." They are in fact sculptural interventions, the →

GRAUX & BAEYENS removed all partition walls from the ground and first floors to create an open plan, to which they then added their "monoliths." The versatile forms divide the space but do not restrict activities within it.

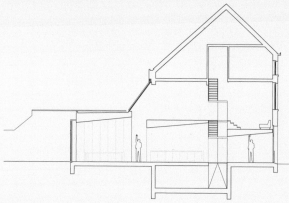

wall and ceilings of which are angled in order to create a slightly distorted perspective. Each of these interventions defines a function, either underneath it or above, without compartmentalizing the space. Life happens around these three building blocks and from wherever you are in relation to them, you have a full

appreciation of the other volumes as well as a view onto the garden.

The original facade was almost totally retained with the only intervention being the semi-transparent pivoting door for the bicycle atelier and the entrance door, which contrasts with the rough facade. _____

An Industrial Workshop for FAMILY LIVING
Jonathan Tuckey Design

Dates from: 19th century
LONDON, UNITED KINGDOM

THIS IS A TRANSFORMATION
of a nineteenth-century steel fabricator's workshop in North London. The building has no direct frontage to the street, other than a front door and garage. The site is long and narrow but widens at the southern end. The house, as Jonathan Tuckey designed it, is formed of three main elements: the entrance hall and living area, which are entirely top-lit, above which lies a mezzanine; a central kitchen and dining space, located in the refurbished steel workshop that has a bowstring truss roof; and a walkway →

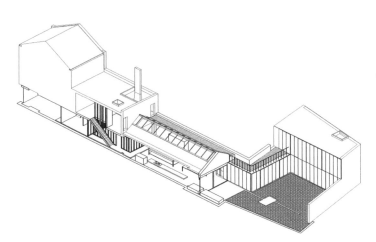

Before modification

Beech plywood sheeting is used as a floor lining, Douglas fir
studs create walls and screens and the exterior cladding is formed
from both operable and fixed larch plywood panels.

Originally a nineteenth-century laundry and then a steel fabricator's workshop in the 1960s, the long and narrow setting proved a challenge to transform into a family house.

linking these spaces to a new two-story structure housing the bedrooms and a bathroom. The dining area and bedrooms overlook an internal court-yard space.

The three elements are bound together by a material palette of three types of wood. Beach plywood sheet-ing is used as a floor lining, Douglas fir studs create walls and screens, and the exterior cladding is formed from both operable and fixed larch plywood panels. Timber studwork is planed and left exposed so that it creates partially subdivided spaces. _____

Letting New LIGHT in
Bernath + Widmer

Dates from: late 19th century
FRAUENFELD, SWITZERLAND

ONE SHOULD ALWAYS

bear in mind that there can be considerable pressure from conservation professionals to ensure that buildings retain their historic appearance after renovation. It is often down to the skill of the architect to reconcile the demands of heritage experts and the needs of their clients. This barn in the hamlet of Dingenhart, near Frauenfeld in Switzerland, is a case in point. The clients wanted as many open spaces as possible with views to the distant Alps. Those in charge of the patrimony of Switzerland insisted it cohere with the context of the peasant village image, allowing only a few windows to be added to the long-abandoned property.

The distinctive appearance of a simple farmhouse and attached barn covered with boards was to be maintained as faithfully as possible. Visible posts and beams structure the interior floorplan while transparent and opaque fillings define the spatial boundaries within the barn. Two vertical concrete structures, inside which the water and electrical appliances are arranged, stiffen the latticework.

The form of the original barn was retained and its structures developed and then left exposed.

Before modification

Transparent and opaque
fillings between the
beams and posts define
the spatial boundaries
within the barn.

MAPPING TIME on Factory Walls
Cannatà e Fernandes

Dates from: late 19th century
GUIMARÃES, PORTUGAL

Before modification

Salvageable elements of the masonry of the old factory were cleaned and reused; sections beyond repair were replaced with white concrete.

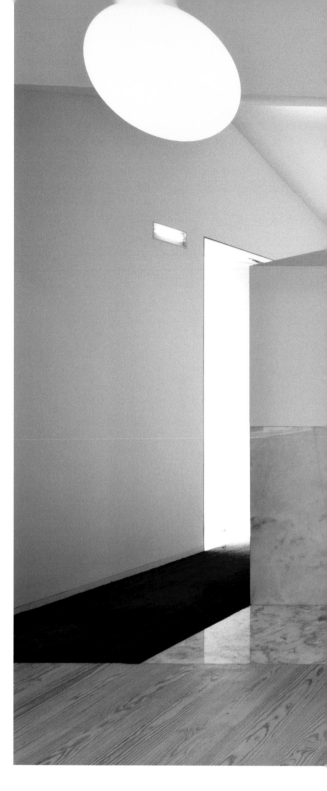

THE LANDSCAPE LABORATORY in Guimarães, Portugal, is a modern restoration of an old stone factory by the Porto-based firm Cannatà e Fernandes. The rebuild has a very clear strategy, reflected in the way the architects employed different materials. The existing elements in good condition, such as the stone walls, were cleaned and then reconstructed, while the dilapidated elements were replaced by white concrete. This was done not only in the brick-walled sections but also used to replace the series of pitched, tiled roofs with concrete structures of the same shape.

On the west side of the building, a large conference room, dominated by the undulating roof pattern, was created by opening a series of smaller units and taking full advantage of the former factory's impressive width. At the east end, facilities such as a kitchen inhabit the original interior divisions more easily. This thoughtful approach makes the most of the original building's important relationship with the adjacent Ribeira de Selho canal. _____

Contemporary Design in a DISUSED WORKSHOP
GAFPA

Dates from: mid-20th century
GHENT, BELGIUM

The corrugated metal roof and the structures of this former stonemason's workshop have been retained for character.

Before modification

THIS TIMBER-FRAMED HOUSE
inside the steel-and-concrete skeleton of a disused stonemason's workshop in Ghent tells the tale not just of the structure but also of the building's function. While the former occupant worked in stone, the new one works in wood. Although the exposed structure of the main part of the house is in steel, the architects GAFPA retained the concrete frame of a former outbuilding and turned it into a walled garden.

Indeed, the new owner was one of the key contractors involved in producing the new building. The →

two-story residence is built within the existing perimeter of the old semi-industrial building. This timber-framed structure was largely built by the owner. The corrugated metal roof was retained for the practical purpose of protecting the new addition from the elements. Few materials exemplify a light-industrial or artisanal heritage as well as corrugated metal, so it is no surprise it was also retained as a reminder of the building's history prior to renovation. _____

Playing with MINIMAL SPACE
AZO Sequeira Arquitectos Associados

Dates from: ca. 1920
SOUTELO, PORTUGAL

Before modification

A disused dovecote in the garden of a family home was transformed into a minimal and magical play house.

"THIS IS AN EMOTIONAL DESIGN," says Mário Sequeira, and it is hard to disagree. When the client invited the architect to survey a derelict stone-and-wood dovecote in the backyard of his home against a boundary wall and imagine a purpose, Sequeira proposed a magical play house for children on the first floor. In addition, he suggested subdividing the structure in order to incorporate a showering area that would complement the nearby swimming pool.

Instead of providing the children with an overtly "childlike" environment, Sequeira says that he wanted the play room to be a place of inspiration. He therefore decided to create a minimal, concrete "tree house," which would gradually be decorated by the children's drawings and toys.

The building itself, although it retains the form of the original, is effectively a total rebuild. The whole structure was created from in-situ poured concrete with the upper section left exposed, which retains the patina of the wooden mold form that produced it. Beneath, the lower level has been clad in recuperated granite stone. But some elements of the original building still remain, such as the triangular windows of the doves. _____

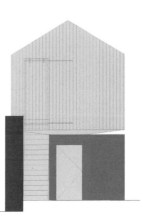

CHAPEL LIVING in the West Country
Jonathan Tuckey Design

Dates from: 1867
WILTSHIRE, UNITED KINGDOM

The additions to the rear of the former chapel were removed to allow for bright open spaces. Working with the slope of the garden, the architects dug down to provide two generous stories.

TO COMPLEMENT THIS BATH

stone and slate Baptist chapel, the walls and roof of the extension were clad in a blackened timber as a direct reference to the tin tabernacle churches, which are a vernacular type of the rural West Country, a part of England to the southwest of London. The blackened homegrown western red cedar timber cladding was used on both walls and roofs and acts as a rain-screen and sunscreen protecting the bitumen board beneath. This detail conceals the familiar profile of gutters, ridges, upstands, and parapets beneath the timber lining, allowing for the refined silhouette.

The extension was planned to retain the aesthetic of the chapel both internally and externally while providing four bedrooms and accompanying bathrooms for their family. The sizable extension meant that the nineteenth-century chapel did not have to be divided and could work simply as a day room with kitchen and living room. From the exterior, the extension effectively appears to be a shadow of the chapel. It was dug into the slope, accommodating two generous stories without rising above the roofline of the older building. ————

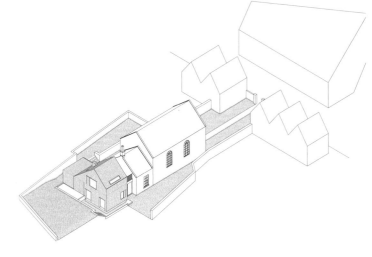

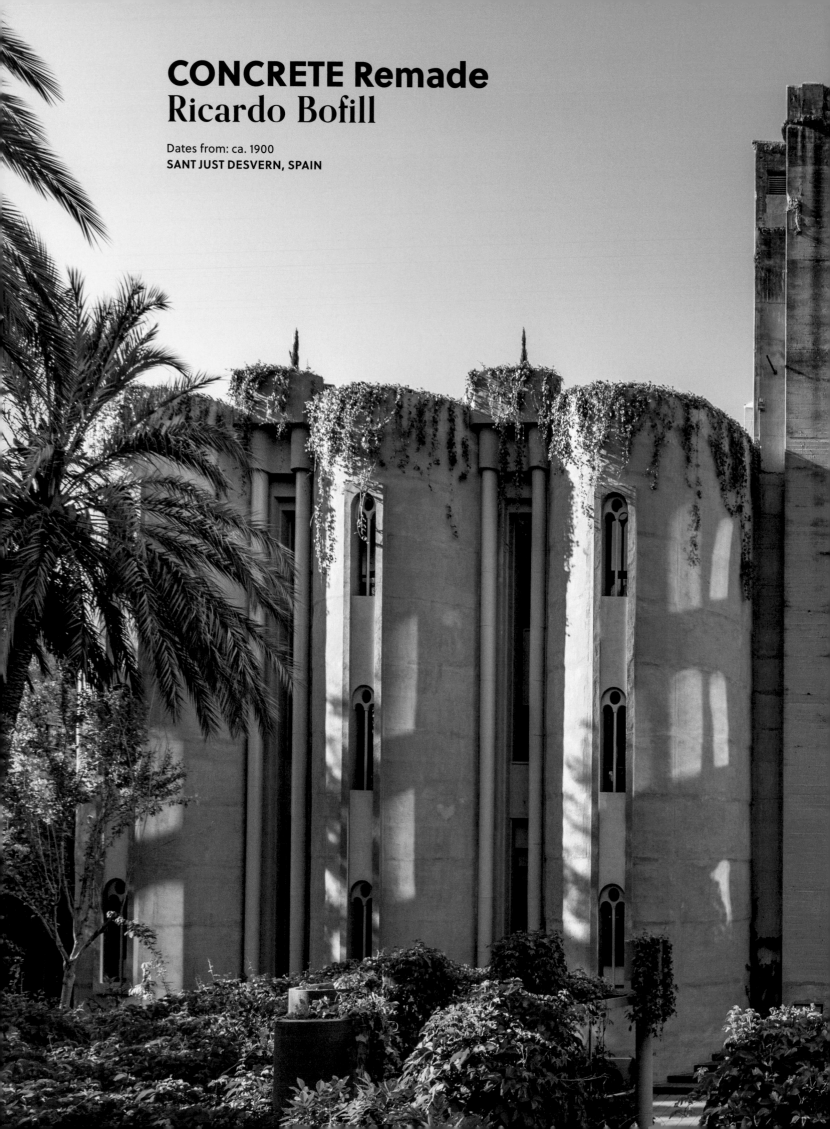

CONCRETE Remade
Ricardo Bofill

Dates from: ca. 1900
SANT JUST DESVERN, SPAIN

Bofill decided to sculpt the factory like a work of art by modifying its original austerity.

WHEN RICARDO BOFILL FOUND La Fábrica in 1973, it was a series of enormous silos, a tall smoke stack, four kilometers of underground tunnels, and rooms full of machinery. The cement factory, dating back to the early industrialization of Catalonia, was not built as a whole but through a series of additions, which addressed various developments in industrial production.

Bofill says he found all the key visual and aesthetics trends of the twentieth century in this factory: surrealism, for example, in the strange staircases that lead to nowhere; abstraction in the pure volumes of the fabricating spaces; and Brutalism →

In 1973, the factory was a series
of enormous silos, a tall smoke stack,
four kilometers of underground
tunnels, and rooms full of machinery.

Layers were stripped
away from the original
factory to expose the
sculptural interior
structures *(right).* The
building was originally
built in stages, with new
parts added as and
when they were needed.

in the abrupt, sculptural qualities of the materials. He decided to use the factory for his practice and to sculpt it like a work of art by modifying its original austerity.

The upper part of the factory serves as Bofill's office, occupied by 40 employees, while a huge volume of brute cement in the main chamber was set aside for his own home. The dining room, located on the ground floor of the building, is the meeting point of family and colleagues. The architect designed a rectangular white marble table on iron supports to act as a centerpiece for the room. _____

Before modification

Interventions with an Eye on the FUTURE
Zecc Architecten BV

BASED IN UTRECHT, THE NETHERLANDS

Over a period of around two years, Zecc Architects converted this former church, antique showroom, and concert hall into a private home.

The Old Catholic Church of St. James in Utrecht was transformed into a spacious house between 2007 and 2009. The church is unremarkable on the facade facing Bemuurde Weerd, where the Old Canal feeds into the Vecht River. The church had not held a service since 1991, and had been used instead as a showroom for antique furniture. A mezzanine floor that had been introduced in the 1990s, so the church could be used for concerts, was substantially modified by Zecc architects to improve the spatial qualities of the church in its renovated state.

Removing portions of the intermediate floor created interesting sightlines as well as allowing light to penetrate better into the body of the church. This logic of light accessing the ground floor through the mezzanine

also dictated the way in which the circulation of the space works through the structure beneath the mezzanine and connects the open front to the rear of the church, where the altar once stood.

Although the church is currently under private use, it was deliberately converted in a manner that could easily reconvert it for public use—as a library, bookstore, museum, or even a church. The original structure has been modified to the smallest possible degree. The existing wooden floor, the stained-glass windows, and old doors were retained and repaired locally. The new, white volume was "kept separate" from the church walls, columns, and vaults. The tight plastered volume is constructed from steel, wood, and sheet metal. Glass surfaces in the volume reflect the

historical elements, which creates a fusion of old and new.

Zecc architects are based in Utrecht, which co-owner Bart Kellerhuis describes as a "historic city in the center of the Netherlands with a unique canal structure." It is also one of the nation's oldest cities, which helps explains the heritage culture in which they work. "Because Utrecht is one of the oldest cities in the Netherlands, we have a lot of monuments and historic buildings. But I think it is interesting to transform them so they can have a second life with a new kind of function. This is one of our main specialties," says Kellerhuis. However, it is not a case of adapting buildings in a quiet, relaxed way. Located just south of Amsterdam, Utrecht is also a modern, dynamic place and "one of the fastest growing cities in the Netherlands." →

We are entering into a new phase with how historic buildings are dealt with in our cities.

While the increasing urbanization of Utrecht is creating a lot of potential for new work, it is also producing a lot of interesting conflicts within the old city. It is in this context that their adaptation of a church into a residential building took place. Significant, too, is their understanding that the building may again be converted in the not-too-distant future, as the momentum of the rapidly changing yet culturally rich city increases.

The senior partners all studied at the Amsterdam Academy of Architecture and the practice boasts that institution's familiarity with marrying architectural verve and experimentation with the practicalities →

of running a practice. But as their work shows—for example, the system by which they suspended a white plasterboard wall from the historic stone of the church—they are also interested in the technical aspect of their profession. "Before we started, we also studied technical engineering. So we know how to build and we have a common fascination for the technical aspects," says Kellerhuis.

Like many architects today, the partners in Zecc took no specific →

During the conversion, Zecc had in mind that the building might soon be reconverted for public use. The design has the potential to work for commercial purposes or even as a church again.

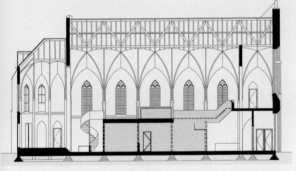

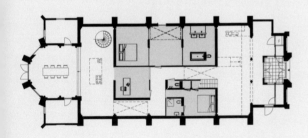

Zecc preserved many of the church's large open spaces and original features. Living areas are modular and could be removed without affecting the structure.

The increasing urbanization of Utrecht is creating a lot of potential for new work.

courses in conservation. Quite simply, the needs of the moment have compelled them into an understanding and appreciation of the building techniques and materials of the past, not to mention how these must be reordered and restructured to create environments suitable to the modern age. Those who excel in their own profession are often obsessive about their area of expertise. Zecc are no different. The interest in renovation, they say, "is purely the result of our fascination for this after our first project in this area."

In many ways, we are entering into a new phase with how historic buildings are dealt with in our cities, largely due the increasing drive towards urban living. "The attitude towards the transformation of old and monumental buildings had to change," says Kellerhuis. "Now governments and municipalities are more progressive towards transformations than ten, twenty years ago." We still want to retain our sense of continuity with our past, but we have changed our attitude about how to do so. _____

ZECC ARCHITECTS HAVE converted a number of water towers in The Netherlands. In the beginning of 2017, they began a conversion in Utrecht for a modern office development. In 2014, they converted a water tower in the De Weerribben-Wieden National Park—a protected nature reserve owned by the Dutch State Forest Service—into an observation point with a spectacular route architecturale.

But their first water tower project, completed in 2004, was in many ways the most ambitious, in that it was meant for residential use. The original structure dates from 1931 but has now been converted into a unique twenty-first-century home across nine levels. Turning this structure into livable space, rather than a business or observation point, entailed letting more daylight in and strengthening the relationship with the back courtyard. →

MULTI-LEVEL DWELLING
at Dizzying Heights
Zecc Architecten BV

Dates from: 1931
SOEST, THE NETHERLANDS

The dizzying internal architecture derives from the inclusion of two new staircases.

The practice achieved this by inserting a three-story-high window frame from the ground up. The installation was done in a manner that would maintain the industrial character of the original structure. On the interior, this was achieved by working with materials like steel, concrete, and glass, which also enabled an effective, efficient layout for the series of small round rooms. The rooms sit one on top of the other over nine floors, while still achieving a real feeling of spaciousness. _____

Various staircases, both existing and newly added, connect the levels in the old water tower. Extra windows have been built in to provide views across the surrounding countryside.

roof terrace

master bedroom

living/working space

sauna

bathroom

kidsroom

play- and guestroom

livingroom

entrance/kitchen

RAILWAY LIVING
Revamped
Zecc Architecten BV

Dates from: 1867
SANTPOORT, THE NETHERLANDS

THE PROJECT INVOLVED
the transformation and expansion of a railway cottage next to the Santpoort-Noord station, only 25 minutes away from Amsterdam by train. The house is indeed in an exceptional position; on one side it is bounded by the railway line that runs between Amsterdam and Ijmuiden, and on the other by the Zuid Kennemerland National Park, which is full of sand dunes and beaches. →

However, the extension of the railway cottage is anything but picturesque. The main house, which is actually raised slightly above the garden, has been abutted by a large volume of Cor-Ten steel. Two sides of the extension are finished with large glass surfaces, which allow broad vistas of the surrounding greenery, while dissolving the bulk of the extension from view when seen from the outside. The old railway cottage has been left virtually untouched, although the remains of numerous renovations were removed, leaving a pure and simple brick cottage.

This old section provides security and simultaneously connects all contiguous open spaces of the house. From the center of the house, one becomes aware of all the spaces, new and old, thanks to long sightlines and a suspended staircase connecting the various floors. _____

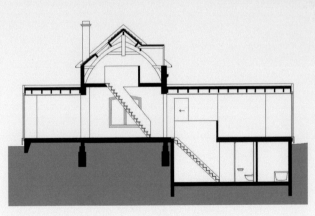

The earliest part of
the house connects
the flat-roofed
sections. A waterfall
staircase links the old
and new sections of
the house.

A COR-TEN Phoenix from the Ashes
Haworth Tompkins

Dates from: 19th Century
SUFFOLK, UNITED KINGDOM

Before modification

THE DOVECOTE STUDIO FORMS part of the internationally renowned music campus at Snape Maltings that has been developed within an important complex of Grade II listed industrial buildings. The studio—for visual artists rather than musicians—inhabits the ruins of the original dovecote and expresses the internal volume of the Victorian structure as a Cor-Ten steel lining. It is a single fully-welded structure, like the hull of a ship, that was built next to the ruin and craned in when complete.

Only the minimum necessary brickwork repairs were carried out to stabilize the existing ruin prior to the new structure being inserted. Existing windows that had decayed were left alone and vegetation growing over the dovecote was protected. Only a small channel to allow drainage was added.

In the Cor-Ten structure, a large northern skylight provides even lighting for artists, while a small mezzanine platform with a writing desk incorporates a fully openable, glazed corner window that offers a broad view of the surrounding marshes, toward the sea. Although small in scale, the Dovecote Studio is a perfect size for an artist-in-residence. _____

A Victorian dovecote made from brick forms the base structure for the artist in residence studio in Suffolk, southwest England.

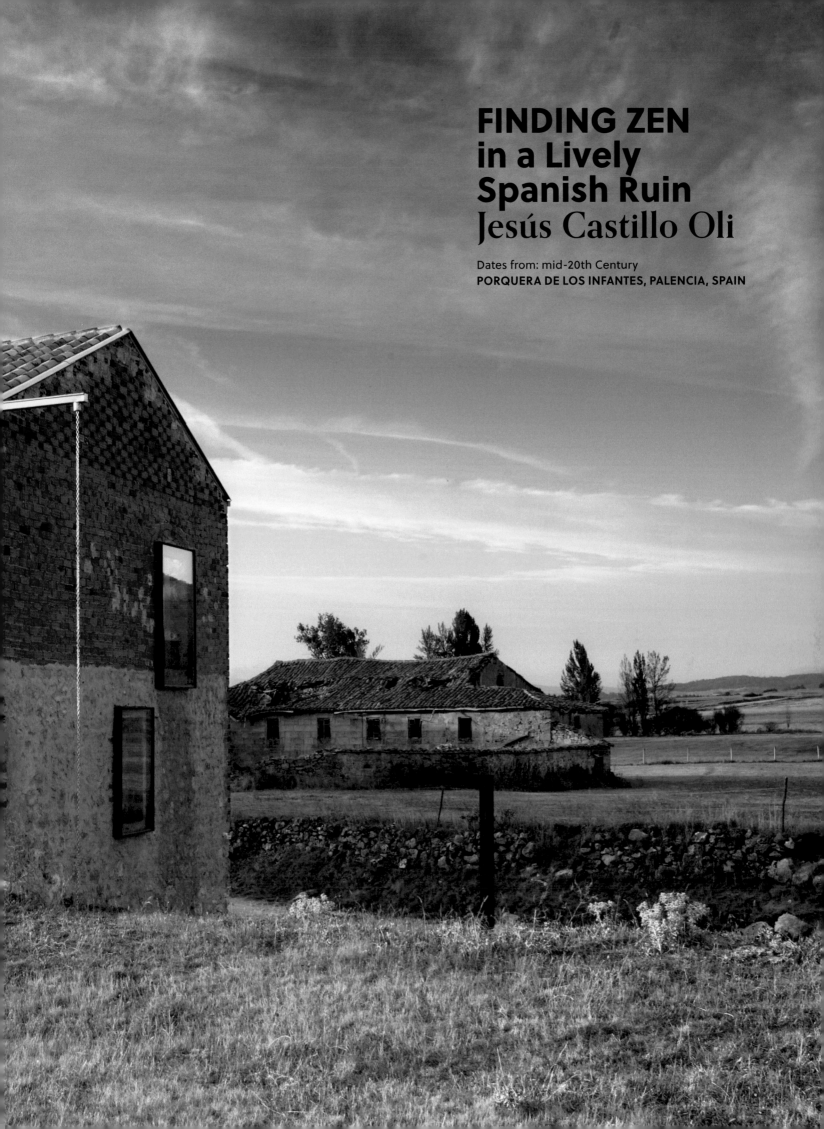

FINDING ZEN
in a Lively
Spanish Ruin
Jesús Castillo Oli

Dates from: mid-20th Century
PORQUERA DE LOS INFANTES, PALENCIA, SPAIN

The outer
space becomes
part of the
interior space,
turning formal
perception
inside-out.

IN HIS BOOK

The Stones of Venice, published in the mid-nineteenth century, John Ruskin celebrated the "mediating power, between the old and the new, and between nature and culture" of ruins. According to the architect Jesús Castillo Oli, the renovated building in this project—an industrial structure in a rural area to the south of Santander in northern Spain—was not in itself of much interest, instead it was the state of ruin in which it existed that was exciting. So Castillo Oli, working for the hotelier Fernando Gallardo, set himself the challenge of imagining how to live in a ruin.

The area where the roof of the Inhabited Ruin—as it is known—had collapsed, was left as a courtyard open to the elements: a porch with no roof, not unlike the *nure'en* in Japanese architecture. Indeed, Castillo Oli opted to lay it out in a Japanese style, creating a private exterior space for visitors to this holiday home. The glass facade toward the habitable section of the ruin reveals the fully refurbished wooden roof structure on the upper floor, while the interior tiled-stone floor reaches out beyond the glass facade. The outer space becomes part of the interior space, turning formal perception inside-out. _____

The building was a ruin, so the architects decided to take this as a starting point for their design.

Before modification

A Farmstead in PRESERVED BRICK
Lens Ass Architecten

Dates from: early 20th Century
PEPINGEN, BELGIUM

VERY LITTLE HAS BEEN DONE to the exterior envelope of this extended farm building in the Pepingen district of Belgium, just to the southwest of Brussels. Upon closer examination, though, one can see that a large square window has been added, with a horizontal window cut into the entire facade of the largest shed. These new openings are evidence that a certain amount of tinkering has gone on with these free-standing angular farm buildings which are a familiar element in the landscape, providing home and office to the owner, a veterinarian, and their family.

A few outbuildings were removed but most else was kept. Rough brick facades and angled beams were not treated as defects, but as details that give this architecture its identity. The facade can be read as the development phases of this farm. The low ceiling was raised so that an extra row of window openings brings light into →

The majority of the existing farmstead near Pepingen was retained, though large new windows were cut into the coarse brick walls. The textured brick, with all of its imperfections, was also kept, as it illustrates the building's history and links the past to the present.

Before modification

the living room. An existing rear door is provided with a window opening, in order to provide a view of an old tree.

Very little was added: an external wall was constructed to close off the building to the street and to create a fully-fledged farmstead with a courtyard. This was not simply a case of making the buildings suit the norm of such farm buildings but also bringing the house together into a cohesive whole. Like an island in a landscape: a landscape permanently altered by the passing of the seasons. _____

In RUINS
Labor 13

Dates from: late 19th century
VERNERICE, CZECH REPUBLIC

THIS LARGE STONE BARN
was once part of a large farm in the Central Bohemian Uplands of the Czech Republic, or Středohoří as they are known. The main farm fell apart during World War II and the barn held out until sometime around the winter of 2010, when the roof collapsed under the weight of snow. Labor13's response to this abandoned landscape was a conceptual project, which created an inhabitable object situated within the ruins and the wild landscape of Středohoří beyond. The structure was built using four principles: construction should be cheap; local materials and labor should be used wherever possible; the border between interior and exterior should be erased; and it should be comfortable but not excessively so.

Fragments of the exterior walls of the barn were preserved creating a semi-open courtyard within which the "object," as the architects call their structure, was placed.

The whole of the south facade can be opened, while the northern gates open onto the courtyard area defined by the remaining walls of the stone barn. The whole building was realized with local material sources (such as timber and the recycled material of the original barn) and by local suppliers. A well and sewage-disposal plant have already been realized. Future plans include the installation of Fotovoltaic and solar panels. _____

Before modification

The rundown barn with
a collapsed roof
provided a setting for
Labor 13's construction.
Fragments of the
original stone walls were
preserved to define the
courtyard and other
exterior spaces.

Additional CONTRASTS
Ziegler Antonin Architecte

Dates from: early 20th century
SENNEVILLE-SUR-FÉCAMP, FRANCE

THE RELATIONSHIP OF AN
extension to the main house is always
an interesting one. We tend to assume
that the extension would be an expansion or continuation of the main house,
but often the purpose of an extension is
entirely different to that of the principal
structure: a place to escape the purely
quotidian concerns of daily living. This
library atop a garage in Senneville-
sur-Fécamp, just north of Le Havre, is
a case in point. Symbolically separated
from the main body of the home by an
entrance stairway, it is a dark, rectilinear
structure that stands in contrast to the
light-colored brick walls and pitched
roof of the original building. →

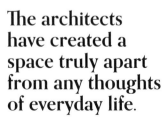

The architects have created a space truly apart from any thoughts of everyday life.

The lower part of the house with a sloping roof was replaced by a structure that stands in complete contrast to the form of the house.

Before modification

The library on the upper floor is a space utterly apart, providing an escape from its frames of reference. The unusual and unique dimensions of the main window on the front facade provide a view across the front of the plot, whilst half-height glazing on the opposite side of the main house keeps one's gaze firmly away from the everyday world. Having abandoned the roof-line of the original house and covered the walls inside and out with wooden boards, the architects have succeeded in creating a space truly apart from any thoughts of everyday life.

A Home Between CONCRETE and Stone

Brandão Costa Arquitectos

Dates from: early 20th century
ARGA DE CIMA, CAMINHA, PORTUGAL

SITTING AT THE VERY CENTER
of the small village of Arga de Cima,
one of the highest points of Serra
d'Arga, in the Alto Minho region of
northern Portugal, this house consisted of a two-story main structure
with no interior staircase to the upper
floor and an outhouse. It is located on
an irregular plot, enclosed by a wall
made of local granite and schist stone.

The design inverts the previous
arrangement of rooms. The ground
floor spaces, partially exposed to the
elements, have been closed and converted into bedrooms. The first floor,
which was originally partitioned, is
now one long, continuous space for
the lounge and kitchen. To compen-
sate for the lack of internal circulation,
a small extension was built to intro-
duce a double-height entrance hall
and staircase.

The need for higher ceilings,
larger spans, and circulation space was
solved with a concrete expansion—
which apart from stone was the only
material used for the conversion and
extension. The concrete has been
placed atop the original stone mass
to fill in the existing irregularities
in the stone and create a new, clean
roofline.

Concrete has been placed
atop the original stone mass to
fill in the irregularities
and create a new, clean roofline.

The original stone and wood
structure only consisted
of the outside perimeter walls
when the work started.

HARMONY in Wood and Stone
Othmar Prenner

Dates from: 1448
GRAUN, ITALY

Before modification

Until the conversion work started, this stone and wood farmhouse was in a state of disrepair, with no electricity or water supply.

OTHMAR PRENNER
is a furniture designer, who studied sculpture in Innsbruck and Munich after undertaking a cabinet-making apprenticeship as a young adult. He designed and built his own barn conversion in his native South Tyrol, Italy and has worked on it steadily since purchasing the property twenty-five years ago. Prenner has re-clad the barn in larch wood, which came from the valley and was specially cut so that the tree's pattern of annual rings would run evenly. A total of 250 square meters of the finest parquet was installed. The large window reflecting the mountain peaks stands out against the dark, textured gray exterior. →

In addition, the designer has reorganized the interior to take advantage of the breathtaking views along the valley. The living area, including kitchen and dining room, was relocated to the second floor. The more secluded and darker ground level is brightened by a white marble floor, with the material quarried just 30 kilometers away, while the master bedroom's en suite bathroom creates a harmony of wood and marble elements. Prenner preserved the old stone staircase—or, at least, its remnants—as a decorative element and a nod to the old structure of the farmhouse. The modern, floating wooden stairs and the bridge—or wooden walkway—to the living room on the second floor create a striking contrast. ―――――

Remnants of the old stone staircase were preserved as a decorative element and a nod to the old structure of the farmhouse.

A Modern BOATHOUSE in Local Timber
Koreo Arkitekter + Kolab Arkitekter

Dates from: 1970
VIKEBYGD, NORWAY

The original boathouse was constructed from wood and had corrugated asbestos panels on the roof. The architects built in folding doors so the client could access their stone terrace on the west side of the former boathouse.

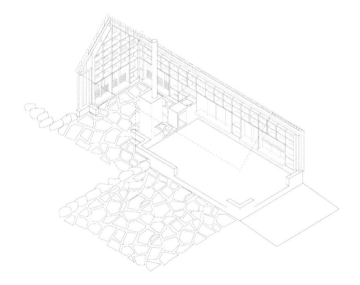

Before modification

ORIGINALLY A BOATHOUSE

—or *naust* in Norwegian—the clients had been using the old structure primarily as a venue for summer parties, social gatherings, and festivals. All the adjacent boathouses were built using simple and rough materials, well-adapted to their exposed position, and the main goal was to make it fit into this context. From a distance it looks like an ordinary boathouse, but upon approach, the uniqueness of this locally-sourced timber structure becomes more and more apparent.

New sections of concrete foundation were added and cuts were made to areas of the existing foundation to accommodate the changes. The renovation keeps the footprint of the existing, including the stone terrace built by the client on the west side. A cut was made in the foundation here, and bifold doors were added to create a transition between the new interior and the stone terrace. The interior is plywood-lined and the walls are lined in polycarbonate to allow light through the exterior wooden screen.

In recent years, the rugged coastline around the Sandnes region in southwest Norway has developed thanks to the oil industry. Today the pleasant, old port of Sandnes is a mid-sized city with 75,000 inhabitants. The outlying districts beyond have benefitted, even as agriculture has become less important economically. Trodahl Arkitekter are a practice that has committed to revitalizing and reimagining the architecture of this rural area, working for clients who are engaged with the landscape and history of the region. The Köhler Pavilion, a richly decorated, notched wooden structure in a typically Swiss style, is a notable example of the work they have been called upon to carry out.

Eschewing Fashion for FUNCTION
Trodahl Arkitekter

BASED IN SANDNES, NORWAY

In the mid-nineteenth century, the original owner had acquired 11 farms to create a prototype for the then-modernizing agriculture industry, and this pavilion was a part of the farm's park facility. After he went bankrupt in 1868, the farm was split up, and the pavilion was used for storage and as a henhouse for many years before it was moved to its current location. Working from one photograph, which depicted the building in its original form, the renovation was as much archaeology as architecture. As they worked on the site, the contractors found parts of the original balcony columns and the cornice of the original roof.

"There is often missed potential in rectifying wooden structures," says Ådne Trodahl, founder of the practice. "But they can be picked apart and put back together and only a few critical parts are replaced. This creates a beautiful puzzle of old and new parts." They are aided in this goal by the diversity of the Norwegian forest. "We have rich access to wooden material in the region, both softwood, conifers, and deciduous wood. This makes working with wooden buildings a pleasing challenge."

The house was actually moved to a new site and set on a purpose-built foundation with a basement and faced with natural dry stonemasonry. The pavilion was covered in ore-pine—a type of high-quality timber cured in a very traditional way meant to resist decay. Decorations on the supporting structures were cut by hand with a jigsaw and all glass work was created by a trained glassblower. The paintwork was done in linseed-oil paint, the same type of paint as in 1860. Long used as a henhouse, it is now used as a gourmet dining facility.

Yet Trodahl Arkitekter are not simply conservation architects. According to Trodahl, the practice is "trying to create uncomplicated and functional houses with a thoughtful integration of daylight. We are focused on the details concerning joining and transitions between materials and surfaces. Typically, the contract budget is low, so we need to think smart to realize our ideas." They always try to use local wood and materials, because they feel that this material palette effortlessly gives the project character. However, they are interested in designing and building anew, in often highly modern architectural idioms.

As Trodahl points out, the professional relationships in renovation work are highly rewarding. →

By sticking to the intimate details and ongoing traditions of architecture, Trodahl find themselves in the vanguard.

Rebuilding is "one of the few areas in architecture (in Norway at least) that still revolves around a direct dialogue between craftsman, architect, and the drawing," he says. The practice itself is small: six people in the office in Sandnes and two in a branch office in Copenhagen. But it is surviving and thriving, having been run in its present form for 16 years. There is an admirably pragmatic quality to their work, even in its engagement with the timeless qualities of buildings.

The often-stunning juxtapositions that the practice generates between a traditional house and its extension, which is typically—at least in terms of its form, if not in construction—highly modern, is one of the many ways the work of the practice resonates so deeply. These, however, are often born of practical considerations. As Trodahl says: "The client usually follows our advice as architects. In the projects that require a major extension of an old house, it is often easiest

to do this with a contrast to the original structure."

And by sticking to the very intimate details and ongoing traditions of architecture, by eschewing fashion, they bizarrely find themselves in the vanguard. "There is generally a greater appreciation for taking care of old houses today than 30 years ago. Now we even have magazines and books about the heritage and conservation of buildings and building techniques," says Trodahl.

MATERIAL
Contrasts
Trodahl
Arkitekter

Dates from: 1845
IMS, NORWAY

THE IMS FARM IS ABOUT
a 30-minute drive from Sandnes, in
a territory that Trodahl Arkitekter
know very well. The rebuild consists
of two parts: a renovated farmhouse,
built together with a newer section
clad in blackened timber. The main
building is known as a *Jærhus*, after
the region in which such houses are
typically found. The farmer needed
a place to change boots and clothes,
so the low shed under the gables, or
skut as it is known locally, was rees-
tablished for use as a rough entrance
and laundry room. Elsewhere, the
farmhouse was restored to its original style and historical character. →

Before modification

The *Jærhus* was
first built from
notched logs.
Trodahl examined
the marks on
these to discover
the positions and
sizes of the
original windows.

The rebuild is in two parts:
a renovated farmhouse, built
together with a newer section
clad in blackened timber.

The new structure on the south side of the farmhouse provides space for the kitchen, dining area, living room, office, and a small loft. The extension is lower and smaller in volume than the existing farmhouse, but also executed with a pitched roof: a kind of monumental representation of the fashionable house shape. In addition, the darker-colored extension suggests a more modern touch, enhancing the contrast between the two buildings and thus accentuating the farmhouse's size and biography. _____

A Restoration with Added MODERNITY
Trodahl Arkitekter

Dates from: 1910
ESKELAND, NORWAY

BUILT AS A SUMMER RETREAT
for a family from the neighboring town of Stavanger, the original summer cabin was a delightful holiday home with touches of art nouveau in the roof detailing. Very much a product of its time, only a foolish architect would try to copy the original appearance. Together with the client, Trodahl decided that the original cottage body would be returned

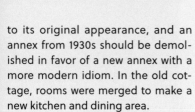

to its original appearance, and an annex from 1930s should be demolished in favor of a new annex with a more modern idiom. In the old cottage, rooms were merged to make a new kitchen and dining area.

The roof of the new extension is green sedum and the bridge, which leads from the exterior through the new building, is made of steel with a slatted wooden floor. The interior features a small bathroom, bedrooms, and a new living room with a double-height ceiling. Like the body of the original summer house, it is based around a timber frame with horizontal cladding. However, in the modern extension the cladding has been painted black. Aspen was used inside the oak floor and internal walls, putting on display the full range of materiality that wood can produce. _____

Before modification

The summer cabin was first constructed in machine-notched logs. Its cladding was hand planed and its foundations were natural stone.

Trodahl and the client decided
an annex from 1930 should be
demolished in favor of a new annex
with a more modern idiom.

Extending into NATURE
Marchi Architects

Dates from: 1890
**LES PETITES DALLES,
NORMANDIE, FRANCE**

LES PETITES DALLES
is a small resort in Normandy on
the coast of the English Channel.
The Petites Dalles—"little slabs" in
English—derive their reputation from
the cliffs that frame the village and
the beach that inspired Impressionist
painter Claude Monet. This building
by Marchi Architectes lies inland, but it
responds to the precipitous drop from
a narrow road into the forest, nestled
primarily below road-level and within
thick vegetation but noticeable from
passing cars by the chimney flue and
accessible from the adjacent property:
a traditional rural French villa.

One of the key roles of the extension was to relate the historical house
to the beautiful woodland surrounding it. The new extension hugs →

One of the key roles of the extension was to relate the historical house to the beautiful surrounding woodland.

the natural slope of the site and large windows allow for views toward the neighboring forest. The volume of the building relates as much to the terrace at the rear of the main building as it does to the road. The house now has a real sense that it is related closely to nature. Thin strips of wood were used on the facade to find a rhythm that would mediate between the trees in the forest and the vertical components of the existing building. ————

SLICING into the Past
Architecten de Vylder Vinck Taillieu

Dates from: early 20th Century
FLANDERS, BELGIUM

JAN DE VYLDER, INGE VINCK, AND JO TAILLIEU ALL STUDIED
at Sint-Lucas in Ghent and have since 2010 created an architecture of the everyday together—or one that at least makes the everyday seem remarkable. Although there is a certain simplicity to their work, its potential sobriety or straightforwardness is punctured by playfulness and wit. None more so than the Kouter II project, particularly in the way it offers an ironic sculptural statement about the family who commissioned it.

The old farm building sits in the back garden of a larger set of farm buildings owned by a family. In this day and age, mortgages for young adults are hard to come by. When the daughters of this family wanted to move out, they were only able to do so by relocating to the property's farm building, which was converted with minimal intervention into their own house, while still being legible as part of the ensemble of farm buildings. →

A simple incision of glass and mirrors brings in light, brings in life, and divides the space inside into separate rooms.

The addition of a new storey creates the necessary floor space. However, the most notable addition is in fact a cut—suggesting perhaps the cutting of the family ties. This incision creates a triangular recess, which is flanked by double-height glazing. As the architects poetically put it: "A simple incision of glass and mirrors brings in light, brings in life, and divides the space inside into separate rooms." _____

Preserving Partitions in a Former Stables
AR Design Studio

Dates from: late 18th century
WINCHESTER, UNITED KINGDOM

WHILE UNDERTAKING
a large-scale refurbishment of the adjacent manor house, the architect Andy Ramus immediately recognized the potential of this former stable block in rural Winchester. The concept was to preserve the existing structure, keeping any additions simple and pure, in order to let the original character shine. In the interior, the preeminent means of putting the historical character on display was by maintaining the exposed timber walls of the original. These were then cleaned, stripped back, and refurbished to reveal their detailing and craftsmanship.

In order to highlight these features, the architect took a more neutral approach to the rest of the renovation, allowing them to stand out like artworks against a beautifully simple contemporary backdrop. Many of the existing features were refurbished and repurposed for domestic use; the original horse troughs were cleaned and converted into sink basins. Being a single-story property with long, continuous views, the layout was tailored and split between sleeping and living quarters, with a central layout allowing for comfortable circulation through the entire building. ____

Before modification

The concept was to preserve the existing structure, keeping any additions simple and pure, in order to let the original character shine.

AR Design Studio decided to retain the original timber partitions in the old stables. These were stripped and renovated to bring out the craftsmanship of past days. The architects also organized the layout of the house according to the positions of the partitions.

From Barn to
RURAL RETREAT
Rural Design Architects

Dates from: 1855
LOCH DUICH, SCOTLAND, UNITED KINGDOM

FEW ARCHITECTS HAVE DONE
more for the revival of interest in vernacular agricultural architecture in their own country as Rural Design. This practice—with its neutral, modernist pseudo-official name—has been revealing the structural clarity and material wealth of Scotland's rural architecture for nearly a decade, bringing them to work in some of the most remote parts of Europe. A great deal of their work is new build, but this refurbishment of a barn and stable block in Loch Duich, near Kyle of Lochalsh on the northwestern coast of Scotland, is also typical of another important area of their work. →

Before modification

Although the interior is entirely new, the overall simplicity of detail respects the earthy and rustic character of the original building.

The building was originally completed in 1855. One side of it was used for storing materials and equipment for a large estate nearby, while the other part housed the horses. The architects were determined to do as little as possible to the building. In their words: "We feel that many conversions lose the essence of the original building." For this project, both the client and architects felt it was important to retain the external character of the original building. Although the interior is entirely new, the overall simplicity of detail respects the earthy and rustic character of the original building. ____

Alpine CLARITY
Savioz Fabrizzi Architectes

BASED IN SION, SWITZERLAND

The exterior stone walls of Roduit House were kept but insulation added, and its timber weatherboarding was replaced with concrete that mimics the wood's texture.

It was the stone construction and the proximity of bare rock in the adjacent ground that determined how Savioz Fabrizzi approached this old rural house, which became known as Roduit House. In Chamoson, not far from Sion in Switzerland, the building possessed a unity with its surroundings, and according to the architects, "a very strong mineral character." In renovating Roduit House, which was constructed in stages from 1814 onwards, Savioz Fabrizzi sought to maintain and reinforce this character, emphasizing the existing stone structure, while using concrete for the parts to be replaced, in order to give "a completely mineral feel" to the whole.

The exterior volume was not changed; the stone facades were preserved and lined on the inside with a special kind of insulating concrete, based on Misapor-brand recycled glass foam. This lining doesn't simply insulate the building. It also forms the new load-bearing structure, which reinforces the old stone walls. Lending a striking, modern tone to the refurbished building, the timber weatherboarding has been replaced by a monolithic wall of insulating concrete with formwork reproducing the texture of the original's timber.

One of the features of the building, which is typical of the Swiss architects' work, is that the old window apertures have been retained. Into these, however, much larger windows were added, increasing the natural light allowed into the main interior spaces, which also allows for improved views of the surrounding landscape. However, this also has an impact on the appearance of the building: the new windows are flush with the exterior, which minimizes their impact on the volume and shape of the building. It also emphasizes and makes good use of the substantial thickness of the walls.

It is a project that is typical of the work by this small, Sion-based practice. For their work in this mountain region, full of abandoned agricultural buildings, Savioz Fabrizzi—comprising only 10 to 15 employees—has developed an impressive reputation for rehabilitating these ruins. "We work on transformations by choice, and we select the most interesting," says partner Laurent Savioz.

The practice has developed an expertise in transforming old farm buildings, in particular adapting them into dwellings. Their work is aesthetically certain. Roduit House is a strong poetic statement about the enduring, timeless shapes →

or forms that communicate the idea of home. "We highlight the historical substance, but we also allow ourselves quite strong interventions on the building. For us the building must not be frozen, it pursues its life with its time ... I think that is what our clients appreciate," says Savioz.

Such ideas can occasionally be achieved by controlling very small details. One of the ways in which the practice highlighted the materiality of the stone walls in Roduit House was to adjust the render between the stones on the exterior walls, thereby emphasizing the significance and materiality of each stone. "The slightly recessed joint gives a roughness to the facade

that contrasts with contemporary interventions. We would not have obtained the same effects with mortar that was flush with the top of the stone," says Savioz.

Making such telling interventions requires a wealth of technical virtuosity, but no less important is an equally broad knowledge of the legal structure determining how historic buildings can be adapted. Anyone wishing to refurbish such buildings for habitation in Switzerland is legally obliged to thermally insulate the new envelope. For this purpose, the practice integrated current technical elements—such as the glass-foam-enforced insulating concrete. →

Before modification

Originally a rural house, Roduit House was built in stages in the nineteenth century. It now consists of three adjacent areas on different levels.

As heritage restrictions vary greatly between projects—and especially by the region in which they are located— the practice must be certain about how this will factor into their strategies. For their barn conversion in Praz-de-Fort in the Val d'Entremont there were no heritage constraints, as the buildings were originally designed to be moved.

However, Roduit House was heritage-protected, so the practice had to negotiate all of the legal requirements. But the architects are comfortable with these limits: "It is right that the authorities give certain rules for the preservation of buildings." And they clearly flourish despite—or perhaps because of—the constraints provided,

respecting the original building and expanding it with purpose, but only when required.

"We have a contextual approach, whether it is a new construction or a transformation," says Savioz. _____

Exposing the Versatility of TIMBER
Savioz Fabrizzi Architectes

Dates from: ca. 1850
LE BIOLLEY, SWITZERLAND

Before modification

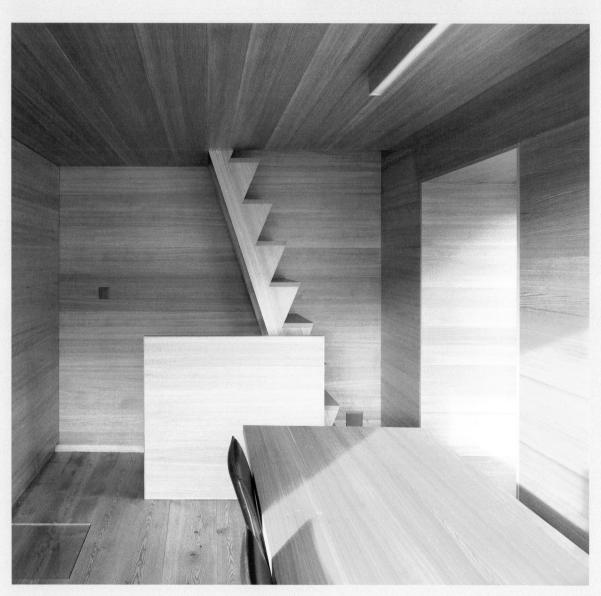

IF THE TRADITIONAL BARNS and stables of the Alpine regions of Switzerland did not already exist, it is likely something very similar would need to be invented. Although many of these were abandoned and unloved for a period of time, the way in which they are now being adapted for holiday residences is incredible.

Indeed, they are the perfect marriage of Switzerland's prosperous winter sports industry with its history and landscape. None have been converted more sensitively than this compact 16-square-meter barn and stable, with a stone base surmounted by a wooden board construction and a gallery for hay storage. →

Savioz Fabrizzi kept the entrance of the converted barn on the middle floor; it leads directly into the kitchen and dining area, which has large windows framing spectacular views. Bedrooms are located on the upper and lower floors.

Converted barns are the perfect marriage of Switzerland's prosperous winter sports industry with its history and landscape.

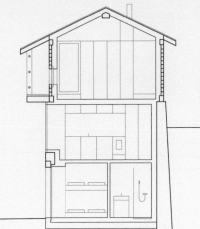

The architects' task was to transform this structure in a way that would take advantage of the surrounding landscape and create a comfortable, contemporary holiday home.

The exterior was left virtually untouched. The entrance on the second floor was retained, allowing the visitor to enter directly into the kitchen and the dining room—the social spaces of the house. This same space also provides a large opening, which offers dramatic views of the valley. The parents of the family were given a bedroom on the upper floor, while the children's bedroom was placed on the lower floor, where the former cattle entrance was transformed into another opening that brings in plenty of natural light.

CREATING WARMTH in Swiss Wine Country
Savioz Fabrizzi Architectes

Dates from: ca. 1850
VÉTROZ, SWITZERLAND

The daytime living areas are located at the top of the building, while the sleeping areas have been placed on the middle level.

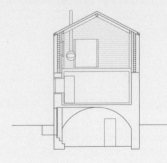

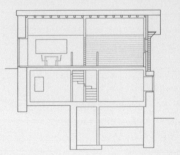

VÉTROZ, NOT FAR FROM SION in the heart of the Valais region, boasts 170 hectares of vineyards. The Maison Germanier, which dates from 1850, was originally the home of a winegrower and stands on a beautifully sunny, sloping site among the grapevines. The house consists of a substructure of rubble masonry with a timber structure above. The stone part traditionally accommodated the areas associated with work and maintaining the land—the wine cellar, tool shed, and so on—while the wooden part provided the ideal premises for the living areas. →

Before modification

The winegrower's house from the mid-1800s combines wood at the top, which was traditionally the living area, and stone at the base, which was formerly a storage area.

The elements of the new project were designed with this traditional division of the building in mind, albeit slightly adapted. The areas used in the daytime are in the upper part of the building, and the bedrooms are on the intermediate level. The varied nature of the structural materials in this building were particularly striking for Savioz Fabrizzi, so they removed the render of the rubble facades and retained the timber. The house is fully insulated inside, with mineral materials in the stone section—namely cement-bonded particle board and cement screed—and organic materials, such as larch paneling, in the wooden section. _____

A Surprisingly Sensitive UPROOTING
Savioz Fabrizzi Architectes

Dates from: late 19th century
PRAZ-DE-FORT, SWITZERLAND

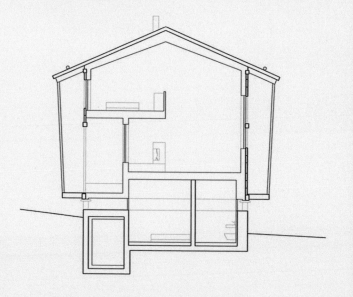

BUILT IN THE SECOND HALF
of the nineteenth-century, this barn was originally situated at the entrance to the village of Praz-de-Fort in the Val d'Entremont, but it had been abandoned. As part of the conversion process, it was first dismantled and then rebuilt a few kilometers further into the valley at Saleinaz. This may sound like an extreme act on a delicate old barn, however these buildings were specifically designed to be moved when needed. At the new site, an independent structure and an internal skin was built inside the envelope formed by the old barn. →

The barn, which dates from the late 1800s and which was abandoned before the architects began their work, was taken down and reassembled a few kilometers from its original site.

Before modification

This separation from the external structure creates a rich spatial mix by allowing open half-stories to communicate with one another. The dwelling was therefore treated as a single open and continuous space, organized through a variation of levels. The bedroom and office, which are the most private spaces, were created in the upper part of the barn, above the living areas and the kitchen. The number of new openings was minimized while the existing door-height openings that gave access onto the different balconies were retained and glazed, creating full-length windows. _____

"ONE OF THE ESSENTIAL
characteristics of the bunker is that it
is one of the rare modern monolithic
architectures," Paul Virilio wrote in the
introduction to *Bunker Archeology*.
But who would want to live in a mono-
lith? To inhabit one, you would need
to break down that structure with
subtlety, using an architecture that is
the opposite of monolithic. Since the
usable surface of the main room is a

mere nine square meters, with walls
measuring less than two meters high,
only the bare essentials for a family
holiday could be added. Taking inspiration from Le Cabanon by Le Corbusier,
the architects conceived modular
wooden furnishing that would maximize the potential of the interior space.

The main room functions as both
living room and bedroom. None of the
carpentry is standard—everything is

custom-made permitting optimum
use of the space. All furniture can
fold or slide away or be pushed up
and down. All objects have a double
function; stools can be used as bed-
side tables, recesses in the concrete
are used for storage space. In contrast to
the hard and monolithic character of
the structure, the architects made their
interventions with lighter materials like
meranti plywood. _____

Modular Simplicity in a BUNKER
B-ILD

Dates from: early 20th century
VUREN, THE NETHERLANDS

The architects conceived modular wooden furnishing to maximize the potential of the space.

A Rustic FARMHOUSE Set in Concrete
Peter Haimerl

Dates from: 1840
VIECHTACH, BAVARIA, GERMANY

THIS PROJECT IS LESS
of a conversion and more of a re-inhabitation of an existing building. The original farmhouse was built in 1840, but had been incrementally altered over the years.

Typical of farms in Bavaria and elsewhere, a single structure had been created to house both animals and humans: barn inside the house, granary in the attic, and hayloft under the roof. The parlor, or *Stube* in German, is the warm core of the building, with bedrooms to the north. →

The new construction frames the old one, carrying it and protecting it, while in turn the old building generously accommodates the new.

For this renovation, the rooms of the old building remain very much as they were, with very little removed. The renovation is effectively structural concrete work, but this was achieved through the recomposition of a number of spaces within the building. Structural concrete prisms were placed in a few central rooms, like the parlor. These were set back from the existing wall to transfer weight from the walls to the ground and foundations. The openings in the old unrenovated facade have been retained. Here, the new construction frames the old one, carrying it and protecting it, while in turn the old building generously accommodates the new. _____

Built in 1840, the Bavarian farmhouse reflects past rural life—it had a barn inside the house, a hayloft in the roof, and the attic was used as a granary.

Before modification

A Stable PARADISE in the Balearics
Standard Studio

Dates from: 1800
SAN LORENZO, IBIZA, SPAIN

ON A MOUNTAIN
in the rugged north of Ibiza lies this house, which was added on to a 200-year-old stable and storage structure, and has now been converted into a showroom and guesthouse by the architects, who also operate an interior design company called Ibiza Interiors that is based on the Balearic island. Particularly noteworthy features that have been retained are the authentic beams made of sabina (or aromatic cedar, as it is also known) as well as the original ancient stone walls in the kitchen and bathroom. The architects only →

Before modification

The original building, parts of which date back 200 years, was used as stables for horses and donkeys.

used materials that were used traditionally on the island, such as iroko window frames, concrete, and white-chalk plastered stone walls.

Although utilities were added, the house is still off-grid, with water coming from a private well and solar panels providing energy not just for water and floor heating but all of the electricity. The building has been designed to become a showcase for the work they sell: Coco-Mat beds, Étoffe Unique upholstery, plus other furniture, lighting, and carpets from their partner shop Modern Vintage. _____

A BUILDING within a BUILDING
Buchner Bründler Architekten

Dates from: early 19th century
LINESCIO , SWITZERLAND

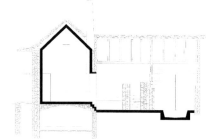

To preserve the original stone house, the architects designed a concrete one within it.

SPARSE, CONCRETE, AND MODERN: The Swiss summerhouse created by Buchner Bründler Architekten is firmly set in the present while being considerate of the past. The original 200-year-old building in the picturesque Rovana Valley is made from granite. On one side of the house is a construction that features a wooden hayloft. The space was once used to dry chestnuts, but is now the bathroom.

To preserve the original stone house, the architects designed a concrete one within it. The interior features lines that reveal how the concrete was cast: layer by layer. The material takes on bold forms and contrasts strongly with the old in places such as the bathroom, where it sits alongside stone and soot-covered roof timbers. The lack of heating, windows, and insulation necessary gave the architects more freedom to leave the exterior mainly as it was.

ILLUMINATING
a Former Barn
Anako Architecture

Dates from: early 19th century
LA FORCLAZ, SWITZERLAND

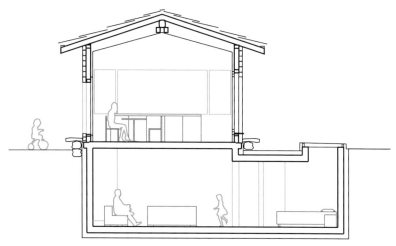

THIS FORMER HAY BARN,
held together solely by planks of wood, has been transformed into a space for living and relaxation while preserving the building's identity, with a facade dominated by horizontal larch-wood beams. Indeed, when the shutters are closed there is virtually no sign of the renovation. The foundation on which the building stands was recast in concrete and a basement extension was added, thus increasing the usable area of the structure. The most significant change comes with the refurbished kitchen, new bathrooms, and →

The concrete floors of the apartment generate
a very special atmosphere in this property,
tucked away at an altitude of 1,700 meters.

The above-ground structure
of the former hay barn has
been entirely preserved.
Windows were placed behind
the wooden boards to provide
a distinctive form of lighting.

Before modification

a full-length glass door that opens directly onto the mountain pasture.

The use of sandblasted concrete for the interior enabled the designers to create a stone-like ambience inside the new basement rooms. The concrete floors of the apartment generate a very special atmosphere in this property, tucked away at an altitude of 1,700 meters. This hut can accommodate two to four people. The new space affords a kitchen and dining room in the former agricultural building. The bedroom is on the ground floor, which is generously heated throughout by a wood-burning fireplace.

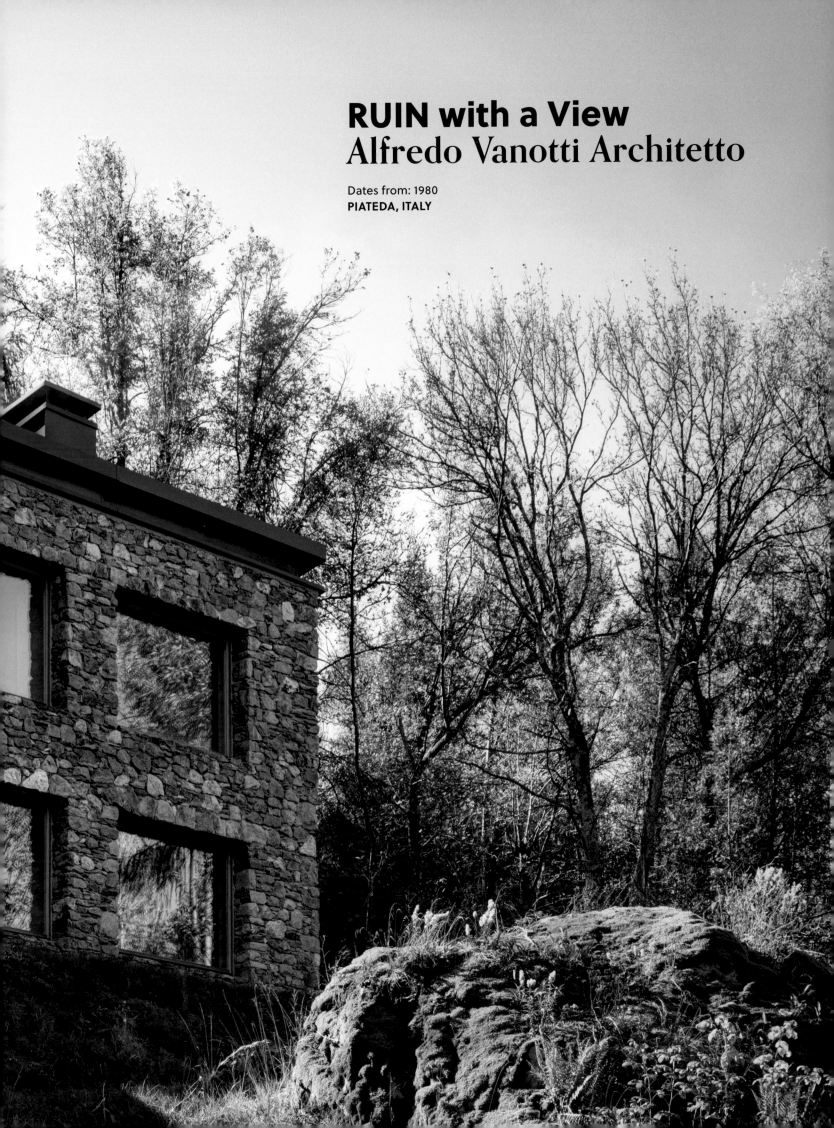

RUIN with a View
Alfredo Vanotti Architetto

Dates from: 1980
PIATEDA, ITALY

THIS HOUSE WAS A RUIN, albeit a recent one: a house in concrete blocks that was never completed. It is, however, in a stunning location, in the surrounding area of Sondrio in the Orobic Alps, at a height of 1,000 meters. But the original dwelling was oriented away from the mountain view. Increasing the quality of insulation allowed the architect to make four openings of equal size on the valley side of the house, providing a wonderful vista of the Retic Alps. At the same time, he achieved double height walls in the open kitchen and dining area, illuminated from above via skylight.

From a formal point of view, the new house refers to the vernacular rural houses: the only sloping roof is completely coated by stone with no eaves. The structure is comprised of reinforced concrete, bricks of concrete with suitable thermal insulation—in order to maintain a good level of heat retention—and clad in local stone. The doors and windows are paneled with untreated larch. The interior is organized by a series of reinforced concrete benches and a staircase, all clad in larch. _____

The structure is comprised of reinforced concrete and thermally insulated concrete bricks, and clad in local stone.

Before modification

The original building sits high up in the Orobic Alps in Italy. When the owner inherited it, it was being used as a stable.

Reincorporating
the CRACKS
WT Architecture

Dates from: 1732
ISLE OF COLL, SCOTLAND, UNITED KINGDOM

THE ORIGINAL HOUSE
in Grishipol, on the Isle of Coll off the northwest coast of Scotland, was built in the mid-1700s. It was the first lime-built, square-cornered house on the island and was nicknamed "the White House," due to its color contrast to the basic black houses with harled walls and thatched roofs, which were the norm on the island. For all its grandeur, the White House was built on sand and was deserted in the mid-nineteenth century as it started to fall apart. The owners, who inherited it, were unsure whether to restore it or to just build a new house. The architects suggested that by partially occupying the ruin they could do both.

A system of exposed stainless-steel ties and bracing frames in the original windows and fireplace openings was devised with project engineers David Narro Associates to consolidate the building. The main cracks were retained and enhanced where possible. A three-story-high entrance hall and stairway was created in the main ruin, with half of it left as a roofless courtyard. A kitchen and master bedroom occupy the remainder of the original building with storage areas, a larder, WC, bathroom and study at its core, all connected by a glass-and-steel staircase. _____

Before modification

The cracks in the building,
which dates from the
mid-1700s, were retained
and transformed into
a feature, as there was
no economic means of
closing them.

The house's main cracks were retained and enhanced where possible.

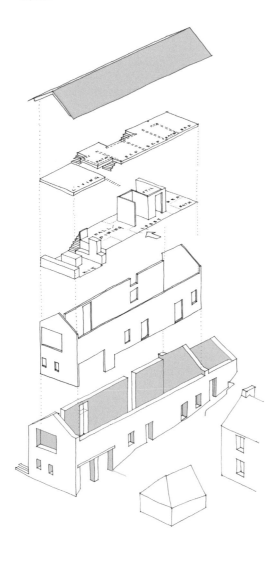

Before modification

A Hillside Home in a MILL
WT Architecture

Dates from: late 19th century
BIGGAR, SCOTLAND, UNITED KINGDOM

ALTHOUGH THE CLIENT WAS
perhaps fortunate in finding a mill in the Scottish Borders so adroitly nestled into a hillside, the architects have made use of the distinctive, lengthy form emerging out of the hillside into a rather exposed position amongst a group of farm buildings. This exposure almost begged for an architectural solution, in which a new property could be placed within the original walls of the late-nineteenth-century mill. As the original roof and floors were beyond repair, a new insulated timber building was slotted within the existing structure. The original walls were consolidated and repaired using stone from the site and lime mortar.

The architects took full advantage of the length and orientation of the original stone walls, which allowed this new structure to extend over the top of the walls to form an ingenious, largely glazed clerestory. Here, the stunning panoramic views of the rolling hills can be appreciated while light spills down into lower spaces. The long cross-section of the site allows for enjoyment of the vertical journey through the building. _____

The nineteenth-century mill nestles into a steep hill. The architects repurposed it as a holiday home and ensured that views were framed in multiple directions.

The long cross-section of the site allows for enjoyment of the vertical journey through the building.

Practical Decisions, Sensitive REMODELING
Charles Pictet Architectes

Dates from: 17th century
PAYS-D'ENHAUT, SWITZERLAND

Before modification

When work started, the living quarters on the east side of the seventeenth-century chalet were in a state of disrepair and the holes in the roof meant there was extensive damage to the interior.

CHARLES PICTET

is a Swiss architect who has performed a number of renovations on vernacular architecture in Switzerland, including a highly praised conversion of an old barn in Landecy. He has also done good trade in all manners of new builds. This chalet in the Vaud canton dates from the seventeenth century and its historic facade is protected by heritage law and therefore cannot easily be altered. The stable and barn on the west side were still in use, though the living quarters had long been deserted. An unrepaired leak in the roof had caused extensive water damage on the interior. →

An important component to the subtlety of the renovation was finding the necessary time to evaluate each conservation decision, replacement, or addition with appropriate sensitivity.

This project consisted mainly of repairs and modifications. Detailed studies were key to the refurbishment. In addition, an important component to the subtlety of the renovation was finding the necessary time to evaluate each conservation decision, replacement, or addition with appropriate sensitivity; these combined elements were the responsibility and the concern of everyone who worked on the renovation of this old farmhouse, which now serves as a holiday home. _____

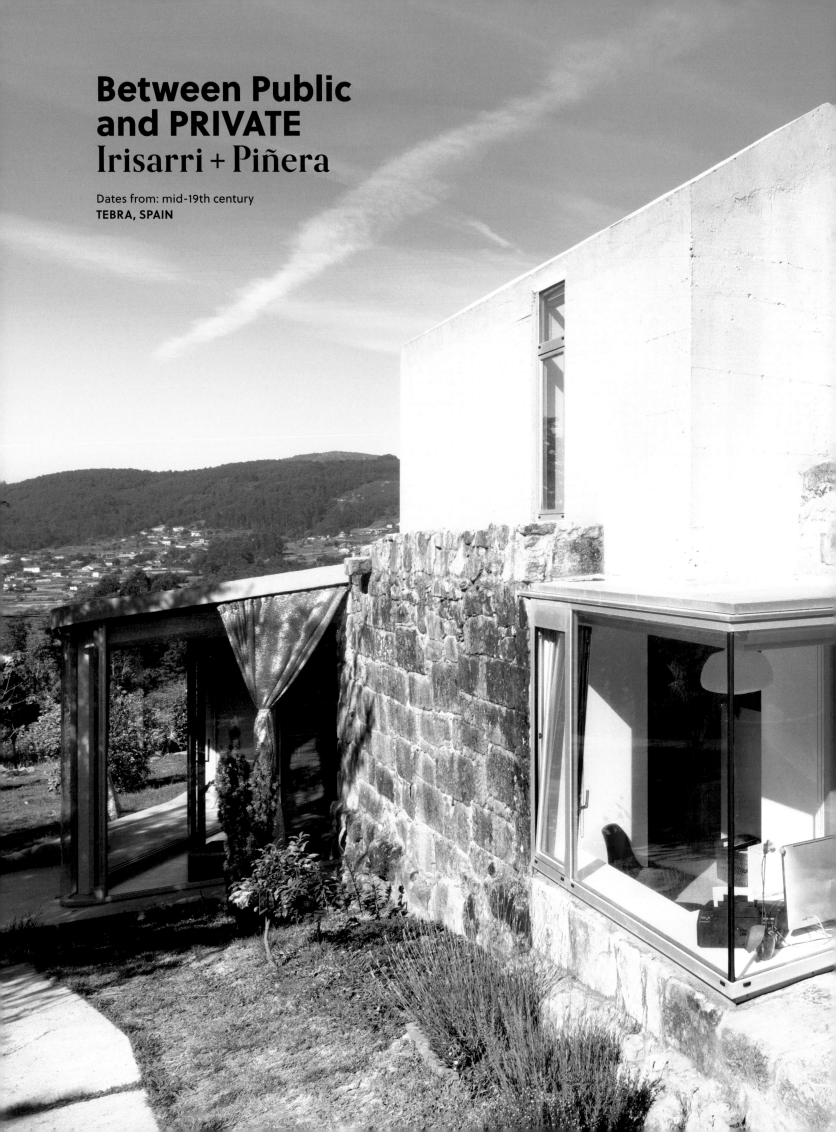

Between Public and PRIVATE
Irisarri + Piñera

Dates from: mid-19th century
TEBRA, SPAIN

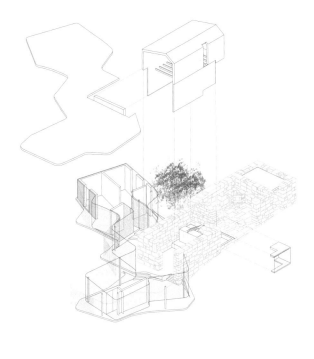

The stone ruin has been expanded using a curvaceous extension. This has formed a string of enclosed courtyards, which provide the occupants with privacy.

Before modification

THE QUESTION IS NO LONGER whether we should occupy the ruins of existing houses but how we should do so. This house in the province of Pontevedra in the northwest of Spain, near the Portuguese border, is an elegant example of how that occupation might be considered in both a pragmatic and poetic fashion. The existing rectilinear ruin sat perpendicular to the road and has been used in its new state to create a series of enclosed courtyards, which create a more private living space. The new, curvaceous extension extends out, running parallel to the terrace, across the hill.

To lift the master bedroom above both the old section of the house and the curved extension to the rear, a new concrete form has been inserted, providing views to the valley beyond and allowing access to the roof of the curved extension, effectively a strong concrete apron introduced to the foot of the old building and supported by columns. This permits the old structure to be experienced sculpturally. The entrance from the luxurious public spaces toward the rear, where the kitchen sits, is one of the most impressive architectural features. _____

Dwelling in BASALT
and Concrete
SAMI-Arquitectos

Dates from: 18th century
PICO ISLAND, AZORES, PORTUGAL

KNOWN POPULARLY AS
"The Black Island," due to the color of its volcanic earth, the Ilha do Pico is a island in the Azores dominated by an extinct volcano—also the largest mountain in Portugal! This occupied ruin sits in a rugged, mountainous region, appearing to emerge from the crust of basalt rock from which its extremities have been built. Dating from the eighteenth century, the old house was small with only a few small windows. The balcony was the only exterior space that permitted the inhabitants to enjoy the outdoors. Because of the steep incline of the land on which the house →

is built, the building must be entered from above. Thus, the architects have designed all the roofs of the new concrete insertion as if they were decks.

On the inside, Sami-Arquitectos retained in some way the typology of the old house by keeping the more social spaces on the upper floor, with beautiful views towards the Atlantic. Accordingly, the bedrooms are on the ground floor, where windows face the interior of the ruin. The openings of the window in the new concrete structure, which was placed within the shell of the old building, are sometimes lined up with the existing window frames and sometimes not, creating new frames and acknowledging the original limits of the house. _____

Before modification

The shell of the old house was small, made from basalt, and had few windows. The stone had developed texture with age and was preserved in the design.

A Restored Modernist CLASSIC
CN10 Architetti

Dates from: 1964
BERGAMO, ITALY

ONE OF THE FEW CONSTANTS in the creative life of the Bergamo-born architect Giuseppe "Pino" Pizzigoni was—according to the author of a monograph of his work—his "intellectual fascination for the mysteries of perspectival projection." Although he studied with Giuseppe Terragni at the Polytechnic University in Milan and became known for his rationalist architecture, he was not wedded to any style. Indeed, his real strength was the finesse with which he worked with a given material, testing its qualities to their limits in the built environment. He experimented with reciprocal wooden frames in furniture around 1948, but soon Pizzigoni became interested in the construction of concrete shells in the form of partial hyperbolic paraboloids, going on to explore this form through the →

The Casa Nani was Giuseppe Pizzigoni's last ever project and captures the breadth of his interests.

construction of complex churches. The Casa Nani—a house built for an artist—was his last ever project and captures the breadth of Pizzigoni's interests. A series of complex roof forms, held in compression as well as tension thanks to a series of beams, Pizzigoni prioritized the views above all else, made possible by extravagant balconies and windows. It has been very sensitively restored by CN10 Architetti, who have gained a strong reputation for their restoration work on significant buildings. _____

Upgrade

Home Extensions, Alterations
and Refurbishments

This book was conceived, edited, and designed by Gestalten.

Edited by Robert Klanten and Caroline Kurze
Text and preface by Tim Abrahams
Project text (page 206) and captions by Amy Visram

Creative Direction of Design by Ludwig Wendt
Layout by Jonas Herfurth and Ludwig Wendt
Final Drawing by Marcel Petersen
Typefaces: Soleil by Wolfgang Homola for typetogether and
Orpheus Pro by Canada Type

Editorial Management by Adam Jackman
Copy-editing by Zoë Harris
Proofreading by Bettina Klein

Cover photography by Giuseppe Micciché
Back cover photography by Michael Pfisterer *(top left)*, Nelson Garrido *(top right)*,
Jack Hobhouse *(center)*, Cornbread Works *(bottom left)*,
Youri Claessens *(bottom center)*, and Michael Harding *(bottom right)*

Printed by Offsetdruckerei Grammlich, Pliezhausen
Made in Germany

Published by Gestalten, Berlin 2017
ISBN 978-3-89955-699-5

3rd printing, 2018

German edition, ISBN 978-3-89955-910-1

For more information, and to order books, please visit www.gestalten.com.

Bibliographic information published by the Deutsche Nationalbibliothek.
The Deutsche Nationalbibliothek lists this publication in the Deutsche
Nationalbibliografie; detailed bibliographic data are available online at
http://dnb.d-nb.de.

None of the content in this book was published in exchange for payment
by commercial parties or designers; Gestalten selected all included work based
solely on its artistic merit.

This book was printed on paper certified according to the standards
of the FSC®.